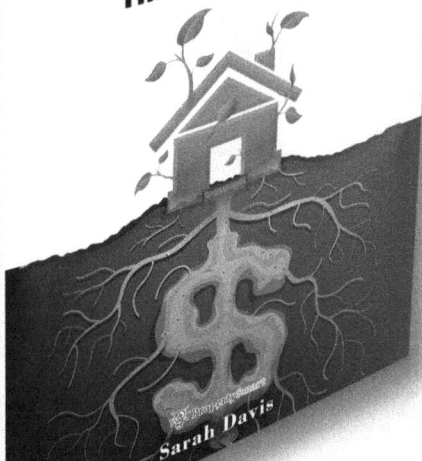

HOW TO BUY AN INVESTMENT PROPERTY

THE SMART WAY

Sarah Davis

How to Buy an Investment Property

The SMART Way

Contents

Dedication

I would like to dedicate this book to the thousands of clients I have dealt with throughout my Real Estate Career, who have given me the experience to write this book.

And my mother, who instilled real estate into my veins, who has tirelessly worked to raise my brother and I, and fellow Real Estate Guru!

Who has her own #1 Amazon Best Selling Real Estate books series;

"Property Success" How to buy, sell or list at Auction

SARAHS
MANAGEMENT
AND
REAL ESTATE
TECHNIQUES

Property Smart

Note to reader *Disclaimer

At no time should this advice be solely relied upon. Every reader's financial situation is vast and varied. You should look to seek professional independent legal advice and financial advice for your individual needs and the current market conditions where you are located and looking to purchase.

This book is a guide to the opinions and ideas of the author, who has vast property investment experience. This book is sold with the understanding that neither the Author nor publisher are responsible for any decision you make following the reading of this book.

Each state, in every country the Real Estate and investing laws are different and each has different tax regulations.

You need to contact your representing professional law consultant, such as your financial accountant, legal representation (solicitor or Conveyancer), Local Real Estate Agent in your desired area as relevant laws to purchasing and investing change from state to state.

The Authors experience is based in Sydney and The Central Coast, NSW Australia. These laws are subject to changes and can be amended at any time. The laws may be out of date to the readers timing. The laws can be reformed at any time and this information is available from The NSW office of Fair trading, and the REI NSW (Real Estate Institute of NSW).
All relevant changes to the legislation is posted through these portals.

Search on the www, for Real Estate Law for your local area to find your relevant state administrator for your specific Real Estate laws.

In this book, the outlined strategies may not suit every individual. These strategies have not taken into account your financial or personal situation. There-fore this guide cannot be relied upon without the readers own research into their individual buying power and local real estate market. The reader is advised to get appropriate professional legal & financial advice independently of this material herewith.

The Author & Publisher make no warranty to the accuracy and completeness of the information provided and hereby disclaim any loss, risk or personal or otherwise incurred debit or financial error following any of the advice, directly or indirectly, it's use or application with any of the content within this book.

The reader hereby acknowledges that their success in property purchasing is guaranteed only by the extent of their detailed research into their own individual and personal situation. The author is not giving any legal advice within these pages.

Introduction

Back in 1989, a hungover Sunday receptionist called in sick. The real estate agency my mother was employed by for the past 2 years, after bringing us from the UK to the "land of opportunity", was short staffed and I was taken to work to help answer the phones.
Being a witty child I handled the job without any issue and was offered the "Sunday girl" position.

I was chuffed to be able to make $30 for 7 hours work, answering phones and taking messages, wages were time and a half the hourly rate working Sunday's, and Real Estate then gave this young girl a cash flow… I was hooked. (I was also very impressed to do photocopying!) And that was the start of my real estate career, although I didn't become a fulltime staff member for another decade, I worked school holidays and nearly every Sunday, and knew I would have a career in real estate.

I purchased my first property when I was 23, site unseen for $66,000. Not from choice, the tenant was never at the unit to view or refused to open the door and pretended not to be home, the phone numbers given from the managing agent were completely uncontactable and the owner nor agent had any spare keys! On my mum's very heeded advice I signed the contract to my first property in the year 2001, 15 years to the day of arriving in Australia. It took me 5 months to get the tenant out, though they did pay the rent, there were 8 single male refugees subletting in a small 1 brm unit, with mattresses on the floor, barely any furnishings and "original" fixtures and fittings is the politest way to describe the unit upon my initial viewing. I probably wouldn't have bought it due to the filth and poor condition if I had seen the property internally when I originally purchased it.

It needed a complete renovation, and they can be costly.

I took possession of the unit and did a complete cosmetic make over. Removed everything, had it completely bare, painted then tiled throughout, I then got a new kitchen put in, bathroom, blinds, light fittings, doors, and made the unit look as liveable, clean and as sterile as possible to attract a better tenant, lucky it was small and the whole job cost me under $12,000!

My mortgage repayments at the time worked out to be $89 per week. The 1st tenant was paying $100 per week so I was in-front with repayments and had money to go towards the strata levies, council and water rates.

Though the property wasn't completely positively geared[1] I really didn't need to put much money into the property from my pocket. After renovating I decided to lease out the unit and the rent jumped to $160 per week! You don't need to be a very clever to work out $160 per week, was a $71 per week pay rise I had just given myself!

I started to get an income from my property, I was being paid to have the investment…. to me; this was "Gold".

As I have always wanted to create a large residual income(2) stream from rental properties to enable my financial freedom.(3) Even back then I couldn't believe my luck being paid to have the loan! I was making money off having the mortgage?! Better than working, even if I couldn't work.. I would still get paid! The market increased and the equity after I did the renovations nearly tripled. By the end of 2003 the unit was valued at $185,000! I couldn't believe it, my buying power(4) had increased so dramatically, I used the unit as leverage to buy my next property and used the equity for the deposit.. I was set.

When you receive a cash flow(5) from a property investment it is called a "Positively Geared" investment. The strength with "Positively Geared" property investment is with the lending bodies, residual income from an investment is a lot more secure than your wage.

You could realistically lose your job at any time and not have an income to service a loan but with a vacancy rate of under 3% (Sydney based) the chance of not being able to rent out a property is very small, so there is a lot of strength in rental properties being positively geared.

This book is a guide through investing in property and will teach you where to look for the best possibilities on your current market and give you a perspective to Real Estate investing that takes years to acquire.

Using the experience of many years of Real Estate deals, (18 years full time!) and my personal trials and errors purchasing investments, you will be able to decipher what will work best for your situation.

Whether you are a first-time investor or are a rental landlord already, everyone will take something valuable from this book to enable them to re-evaluate or fine tune their property investing skills.

I have been helping investors, purchasers, home buyers alike identify their niche requirements and locate the best home suitable to their situation. In that time, I have endured many situations both sides; the good and the bad aspects of Real Estate deals, I will share some stories, some horrors and "Not to do's", as well what is a good buy and how to negotiate the best deal.

Property markets can fluctuate and have many times over the years "burst". This means that the prices kept rising and more buyers fluctuate the market, they force the purchase prices to heighten to a price that cannot be sustained with global economies and the housing "bubble" bursts. The prices decrease under the most recent values or sale prices. Being caught out in this kind of market can be an expensive error. Though you cannot foresee these changes 100% learn what signs to look out for and how to avoid falling into a "bubble" purchase.

Learn how to avoid the miss-haps of property purchasing, property management and leasing errors.
Learn to secure your property investment, increase its worth and get the best return.

With a world that could revert back to economic turmoil like in the 2008 GFC (Global Financial Crisis) at any time, many potential investors are at risk of making poor & financially crippling

choices from bad advice from property spruikers or get rich in property schemes.
Make no mistake, there are no get rich quick schemes to property investing. Property investing is about patience, clarification, the right research and maintaining the home's value while growing its equity.

There are investors who "Flip" homes; buy, renovate & sell. This has been a large growing trend over the past decade due to TV Renovation shows, and most sell at the end, like "The Block" has shown the general public there can be a lot of profit renovating an old property then selling.

"Flipping" for profit is a faster turnover, less equity growth and no rental income used to increase buying power. You are more at risk of losing in the short term, when spending capital on renovating. If the house prices become stagnant or recede, it is very easy to over capitalise, (spend too much on renovating) I have seen buyers sell at a loss if the market turns, house price bubbles burst and the prices come down a %, the potential profit margin was entirely gone and the renovation was more than the difference in price when eventually sold. The home came on at a high price as the other property prices fell and the end cost of all expenses could not be achieved. There are other options but this is a real estate avenue of investing which won't be discussed in this book. I must mention a warning; in short; the taxes are a lot higher when selling a "Flip" property as Capital Gains Tax[6] (CGT) comes into account. This means that the profit you make will be taxed at a higher rate, and as a 2nd income or similar. In Australia, the Capital Gains Tax is 15%; married or high income 20%, if you sell after 12 months of ownership. The CGT is approximately 50% if you sell within the first 12 months. (Check with your financial professional for your direct country & state taxes and rules).

CGT applies to rented investments also, though you are not cashing in on the equity by selling the property, you are using it (your profit and the tax due) to build your buying power, but more on that later.

Purchasing for investment property equity growth is the purpose of this book and its contents.

A fact is a lot of property investors fail, or become financially strapped.

93% of investors stop at 1 or 2 properties. Only 2% of the property owners own 4 or more properties.

To become financially free with property; you will need a multi-million-dollar property portfolio.

This book will detail my experience "How To" set yourself up to purchase your first investment & placing the first paver to owning your own multi-million-dollar property portfolio, the second book show you how to and becoming financially free through property investing by growing a profitable property portfolio.

So, let's start setting the paver on your path to financial freedom….

Chapter 1

Purchasing a Property

Which property is best?

Well the hype is "location, location, location" And IT IS all about the location, ideally locating an investment that's rental yield will cover the mortgage!

The average investor I have dealt with over the years is far from a millionaire when they started. They are normal mums and dads, looking to secure their future with a 2nd property, super paranoid if the tenant vacates as they have no excess income to cover the 2nd mortgage, and will financially struggle if the tenant doesn't pay or vacates and there is no return.

They generally don't have much money to do repairs or maintenance either. These investors are not the multi-million dollar investors, and they never will get to financial freedom the way they use their equity.

These are the average property investors / landlords.

This means that the average property investor today is not whom you should follow. Investors with over 4 properties are the top 2% of investors set for financial freedom.

So, if you take advice from the average investor you will only get the same results.

My purpose for writing this book is to inform those who want to use their equity as leverage to secure themselves a property portfolio that will survive the times, financial crisis, mortgage rate inflation or high vacancy rates. This book uses different techniques to "the norm", a more sustainable plan allowing maximum growth in a shorter timeframe with less risk.

I am not claiming to know everything there is to know about Real Estate Investing, I am sharing the information and experience I have, that has yielded success and great results for my clients.

The location of your investment and securing a rental return that covers the mortgage is paramount. Having a property that can potentially yield a dual income [7] by way of building a granny flat or converting an area into a self-contained flat for a 2nd income.

When I first started in real estate the "gurus" were talking about negatively gearing [8] your investment for tax purposes!

This means the properties income costs you out of your pocket in expenses like the balance of the mortgage repayments, maintenance, repairs, rates, etc. This out of pocket costs can then be claimed as a tax benefit for your personal tax, as it is costing you to house someone else (depending on your states tax regulations). Ideally this is a tax benefit as you will pay less personal tax as your income received, less your out of pocket expense, is your new taxable amount (seek your own personal and professional accounting advice).

The issues with negatively gearing the property in my opinion is:
1. If you don't earn that much money the tax you are saving is minimal
2. The property is now hindering your affordability and buying power with a bank or financial institute
3. It is actually weakening your buying power and you are now seen as a higher risk, if you lose your (job) main income you will not be able to sustain the loan on the rental income alone.
4. If the tenant vacates or the property is empty you will be required to pay the full mortgage and this will leave you financially strapped or ruined until you get your next tenant.

My RULE:
The property needs to be positively geared! If you ever want financial freedom you need to be

receiving an income off the rental yield after expenses are paid.

A purchaser looking to invest in property for financial freedom needs to declare the amount they need.

If it's decided that you could live off $1200 - $1500 per week rental income, and every property you buy & set up gives you an individual cash flow after expenses of say $250 per week, you will need to have 5- 6 properties (10 -12 rental incomes) in your portfolio to accumulate that financial freedom and live off your investment income.

You see if you need to pay anything towards the mortgage to make the repayments you have bound yourself to working in a job to make the balance of the repayments to the bank.

That is the TRAP.

Making extra money today, paving your way to financial freedom and rental income security is the plan. Paying a higher tax now should be seen as no issue! If this secures an opportunity to quit work. No more 9am-5pm, 5 - 6 days a week… isn't that the dream.

If you secure the right homes in the right areas with the right tenant and the right return, you will be able to retire right and live off the excess rental income,

Being financially free to me; means being paid regularly and not having to go to work to earn the money that supports you.

Paying a higher tax now to set yourself up to retire early is the smart choice, positively geared investments are the only way to go to potentially set this up.

More information in the second book; How to BUILD a Property Portfolio, The Smart Way – Where you will learn how to set yourself up for financial freedom. (Book 2 in the series)

Analyse real deal potential

When a property is the real deal – I look for
- ➤ one of the cheaper homes on the market
- ➤ doesn't need too much work,
- ➤ mainly cosmetic improvements,
- ➤ can easily be rented,

- ➢ Will attract a decent tenant
- ➢ is median size home for the demand of the area,
- ➢ has good rent return potential,
- ➢ offers potential to have a second income,
- ➢ looks like a long-term family home
- ➢ Clear block & structurally sound
- ➢ Block is above minimum allowed for 2nd dwelling

Most Real Estate sites on the internet these days allow you to easily research the local area's median sale price, rental amount, growth over 5 & 10 years of the sales market.

Researching the cheapest homes in a good solid community is ideal for an investment, close or nearby to schools and shops. If you are going to the outskirts of a major city and are looking for a stable infrastructure, as a rule of thumb look for sub towns that have city like amenities. For example, towns with hospitals, universities or who are manufacturing produce like a farms or large industrial areas. These potentially create jobs and always have a steady flow of people looking to rent.

When looking at vacancy rates[9] for a specific area obviously less is better. A steady vacancy rate of 5% or under for any town is average & a good % rate. Anything over 15% is a risk as that could potentially mean there is more supply than demand.

When working out your property feasibility chart (10), you will account for a change of tenant each year and 2-3 weeks vacancy for in-between tenancies. This is a farfetched amount in comparison to a normal rental with the average tenant the lease changeover is roughly every 2-3 years. If you aim for a family tenancy with growing kids who need a stable schooling the average tenancy with a family of school kids is 5-6 years. It is a lot harder to move with kids, it can be a tedious and monstrous task, so aiming for tenancies to families usually secures you a tenant for a longer duration. You don't want to be searching for a new tenant every year.

The wear and tear on a property is accentuated when a property turns over a lot of tenants moving furniture in and out, pictures up & down on walls, depreciation of newly renovated areas or appliances.

Chapter 2

Know if the property is sound:

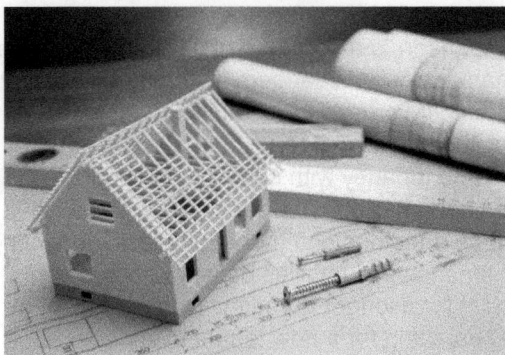

Building / Pest reports

One of the most important pieces of advice when purchasing a property is to get a professional to inspect the home for structural issues like a builder. Make sure the property has no hidden issues that aren't so obvious. Some issues can be seen with the layman's eyes, but others can be hidden within the home, like piers that have moved causing structural movement or roof rafters are sagging and the bearings need supporting.

A licensed building inspector will also check that the home is up to code. Each country has their own safety standard code for building and structural restrictions, some areas are individually set by local council. Using a local builder is advised, as they will know the area quite well, they will know common issues or problems to look out for in this particular area, or will know standard afflictions that occur in that town, such as earthquakes or ground movement during droughts and the like.

Using a local building inspector should set you back approximately $300- $500 depending on how much he extensively details in the report. It will include photos of any areas of concerns and standardly he will quote an approximate guess-timation of the costing to rectify this work.

The building inspectors quote will usually be a loaded figure / cost to rectify any issues. This is due to the buyer being able to come back after purchase and hold the builder to the price quoted if they have based their decision to buy on his report and the work requires more than he estimated. If the estimate is more than a certain percentage they buyer may hold the builder responsible for the difference, due to this they standardly increase their "guess-timate" to avoid this occurring.

You are always best to ask another builder to look at any work and get a second opinion and for a quote. Get an actual price for the scope of work required for structural or cosmetic work.

In my experience, a building report will pick up everything that you can see, and you are buying the house as you see it. Therefore, if the building report comes back saying $20,000 to replace the kitchen, this is not something you can re-negotiate into the sale price. By all means you can mention it in your negotiating, though be aware that the listed sale price is usually indicative to the fact that work is required to get the home cosmetically liveable.

In saying that though, in a buyer's market (11) there are more homes and stock available for sale than buyers looking to buy, and sellers get desperate. In a buyer's market the buyer has the upper hand and can use any means to negotiate the price down, quite considerably.

If, however it is a seller's market, there are more buyers available looking for a property than homes ready to sell, you will need to negotiate fast & strong in a seller's market or you will risk losing the property to the next buyer. Trying to renegotiate (due to a building report) at after signing a contract could cost you any deposit you have put down to secure the home, and the sellers has the right to decline and sell to the next buyers waiting if your re-neg on your offer, and don't proceed.

If the issue was an unseen circumstance, and the vendor(12) was not aware of the issue this could be grounds for renegotiation for the total of the improvements such as structural issues, leaking roofs, & Termites.

Termites are a huge issue in Australia's with such a dry continent, and large heavy rain fall, and we have over 300 species, though only a handful cause problems. Termites will gather and nest in any moist area where timber is exposed or touching the ground, where the termites can climb up from the ground, though Alates are winged termites, YES Termites can also fly, they swarm out of the nest to establish new colonies. They are the king & queen reproducers, and can create a colony of hungry

Termites that can undermine any timber structured home to such a degree wood becomes paper-like and crumbles upon touching.

Professionally trained termite pest inspectors are required to carry out a comprehensive inspection. Also costing anyway up to $300+. This is a highly advised report to get done.

Your legal representation will usually advise what inspections are required or recommended for your purchase area. Some are borer ants, or grubs that eat wood. Check with local pest guy for the specific pests that cause issue in any area that you are buying into. They will usually tell you this information over the phone and possibly do inspections and remedies for the afflictions, and can be appointed to inspect the home via the agent's details.

Some countries such as New Zealand have a compulsory test for Crystal meth (street drug: Ice) & Amphetamine (street drug: speed) residue. As there have been issues with families moving into rental properties which have been used as drugs labs and suffering long term effects of breathing in poisonous fumes.

A landlord is responsible for providing a safe environment, so if you suspect an odd odour in a property you are purchasing: get it tested. The last thing you want is a sick tenant suing you for respiratory failure or any other health issue resulting from them living in your investment.

If you can't find a local who can test for these residues, there are DIY tests you can order online for approx. $25. If you can't find a test, and there is rumour a meth lab or similar, or neighbours claim it was a drug house pass on the property! ..and look for another potential investment to buy. If there is a funny smell, unless the price is dirt cheap, it can cost thousands to chemically neutralise toxic odours that have been absorbed into the walls and carpets etc. at worst replace ALL gyprock. (plaster board. Ie; Walls, ceilings, cornices)

I advertise that I will carry out amphetamine tests in my rental marketing, to deter drug addicts from even applying for my properties. If they know they will be held accountable and have a habit, they will look elsewhere, which is my aim!!

I have seen cases where a tribunal has ordered $54,000 damage for meth contamination to a rental property to the tenant. If anyone can tell me how to get $54,000 from any drug afflicted tenant I would love to hear from you!! Even if it was a meth lab and they have made thousands, it won't be in the bank, Insurance IS A MUST.

What inspections should be done

Pest inspection	ALWAYS!
Building Inspection	ALWAYS!
Drug testing	Optional
Valuations	At banks request / Optional

Valuation.
This may be required from your bank to secure the loan application, and make sure you are not paying too much for the property as they are funding the purchase and seek to minimise any chance of loss to them.

You can pay for a professional valuer to inspect the home. They are licensed and trained at university to speculate on a home's actual value against the sale price, and based on their professional market research and speculator forecast in the current market they will establish if the price is fair in the local market by using comparable sales and report back to the bank or yourself if you have ordered the report.

When purchasing a property at an Auction, the bank will usually deem the highest winning bid to be the accurate market value as it was listed by public auction and the current market was able to fairly bid, therefore depicting the public value. Though I have seen a valuer sent out to a home purchased at Auction. There were no issues in the end, but sometimes if the buyers seem risky the bank will ensure they have a secure asset for the borrowings lent.

The valuer will also take into account many variables and may come in under market value. I have even had one valuer call the broker to ask if they wanted the valuation to include the granny-flat (which was fully council approved & leased!) as it was on piers and he felt could be relocated>???? So, there are morons out there! If a valuer has done a deplorable job, complain and get the bank to send a 2nd company, it is surprising how much they can differ in opinion and don't forget it is an opinion, and like any job skill some are less able / professional!

Builder: Get an estimate of work needing to be carried out for any cosmetic improvements needed.

What to look for?

Structural issues, anything that could cause to be a costly improvement & any Pest Damage.

Ceiling leaks- if there is apparent mould on the ceiling it could be caused from an internal issue or external. If you can see the beams in the roof – clearly not having any mould – like stripes across the area, then the moisture is coming from the inside of the roof, there is rain or moisture getting into the roof cavity and causing the mould.

If the area does not look to have the beams apparent, the leak is likely inside, in my experience it has been a faulty or non-existent exhaust fan to the bathroom. This causes the steam to settle in the home if windows aren't opened. It can't escape or dry and will leave a moisture stain to the bathroom ceiling or hall or closest bedroom. This can be removed with bleach and repainted, then add a fan to the bathroom, that turns on with the light, is recommended. Not a costly repair.

Shower trays are more common to leak also, checking the rear wall of the shower for any water damage. If the bathroom is going to be renovated then this will all be rectified during improvements, but if the water has been leaking a considerable time the floor under the shower could be compromised, timbers could have rotted and need replacing. If you see a leak, get your building inspector to check under the home for structural damage.

Drainage, could be a costly exercise if not properly established. Looking for areas that water can pool or gather, ground that is very moist and it hasn't rained recently or down pipes that aren't connected to a stormwater pipe could need the whole area dug up and re-piped. Keep an eye out for any drainage issue, and have your inspector check any concern you see.

Realistically the building inspector should and would pick up all of the above concerns in his report, but we are all human and make mistakes or miss things, having a 2nd pair of eyes just checking problems areas can help and minimise issues later.

If you don't know what to look for... well that is what you are paying him to do, so relax & read through his report with him or your legal rep., discussing any issue's he has raised and ask if it should cause any concern.

Calculate cosmetic issues and renovations required, what work needs to be done to make this property "pop", and become highly desirable, ideally an appealing liveable investment. Most importantly stay within your budget.

Budget the scope of work

You will need to access funds to do home improvements after purchasing the home. Maybe you have trades people in your family or friends circle who can help with the improvements at a cost price, otherwise you will need access to at least $20,000 to $50,000 for the average full home makeover including kitchen & bathroom replacement, ensuite & laundry, landscaping or repair work.

This usually cannot be consumed into the borrowings of the home unless a separate home improvement loan is requested. This then is paid in stages as the work is carried out, with the bank paying the builder directly to ensure the home is being improved, therefore improving the homes equity and the bank's asset.

This is also the case with granny flat or a building extension loan. Based on the end return, the cost of the scope of work required maybe able to be borrowed and added onto your total mortgage. This mainly depends on your bank and borrowing capacity. Seek a financial professional / loan broker to find out your best options.

It costs nothing to get a home loan quote from a mortgage broker. They will be able to locate the best loan on the market with your specific income and affordability details. A broker will give you multiple options of loans and % rates that are available.

Calculate what available funds you have for the renovation and who may be able to help do some of the work to help keeps costs down. It is very easy to over spend when renovating. Remember you want it to look nice for the best cost-effective price. DO NOT GO CHEAP. It will look cheap & not last. Try to get good quality at a bargain price, I get ex-demo, display baths for less than half the asking retail price. I have also sourced 2-year-old kitchen cupboards in perfect condition, changed the handles and added a new benchtop. A brand new for a fraction of the original quote.

There are also nifty ideas on renovation shows, so keep an eye out for innovative ideas and cheap solutions when renovating.

And stay within your budget! Don't forget, you have an allocated amount to complete the renovations, make sure you have added the outgoing costs such as the banks monthly repayments into that figure.

It is best to set aside 3 months of repayments, to ensure the mortgage repayments are met during the renovation process. Factor in any expected payments prior to receive any rental income. If you finish early you will have extra in the budget.

Chapter 3

Estimate a properties worth

Measure the potential return

The easiest way to find out what the potential returns for rentals are in the area you are looking to invest in, is to do a little market research for that area.

The best way to estimate current rental returns is to do a search for similar home in the rental section of a real estate search engine. Look up the homes for rent in your chosen area and also search for the top of the range for 1 bedroom less and also search for one bedroom more.

For example, if you are considering a 3brm home, look up 2-4 brms, that way you will be seeing what the competition is one the market. Imagine you are a tenant, which would you choose. Price is obviously a main factor in a tenant's decision making, but if you could have creature comforts for an extra $20, like air conditioning – Would you pay extra? Yes, and so would they. The cleaner, newer and more mod cons that are included in your rental the more chance you will have finding a better grade tenancy for a longer period.

For far too long the opinion of the average Landlord and Agent is that tenants are a by-product of investing! Let's get real.. they are the PRODUCT. You are offering your home to attract a good tenant to help you pay off your investment, they are not a second-grade factor in this, they are your team member.

If a tenant isn't happy, comfortable, and enjoying your property you can guarantee they will have issues, complain a lot, move out at the end of 6-month lease or even stop paying rent, and hence problems start.

Put yourself in the tenant shoes, imagine you are your tenant. When you first move into a home there will be some issues that need to be sorted, every home has its little idiosyncrasies that each new occupant will find out over the first week or two. Paying attention to what issues are at hand and assisting a tenant to comfortably settle into a home is a top priority of mine.

I'm the tenant, I've just paid nearly $1500-$2000 in a deposit bond to rent your home, paid 2 weeks rent in advance and now am packing & moving a truck worth of my belongings into your home. There are probably some light bulbs not working, maybe a tap starts dripping, dishwasher may not drain properly, door and locks may need attention, there may even be some cleaning that the previous person has left and I'm now tired, moody and broke.

Most landlords get quite upset in this first week, the tenant is seeming to be complaining about everything, when they are simply asking for a few things to be rectified, the usual complaint is "oh are they going to complain like this the whole tenancy?" > totally the wrong attitude for any investor, they are settling into a new home and would like things to be done as they have just paid for the property. This is a standard attitude, that seems to be instinctive: when we have paid for something…we expect it to work properly!

Showing the tenant at this early stage that you are attentive to their needs, available to discuss any problems and willing to assist or help sort them out any issues, is showing the tenant that they are a valuable part of this arrangement, their needs and comfort is important to making this work properly.

This will also give them an onus of responsibility, they are obligated now to also be attentive to any issues and keep up their end of the bargain> pay rent on time and look after the home as if it were your own.!

As with any arrangement, if both parties seem to help each other and look after the other parties' requirements then there is an obligation to do the right thing.

A tenant is actually you & I! Each and every person, pre-purchasing their own home needed to rent first. I have also had a handful of tenants that are actually landlords…! Home owners who lease out their property, yet rent where they need to be; The Rentvestor!

Clearly, the best home on the market is one that is newly renovated, clean & homely, with mod cons such as heating, air con or a dishwasher etc.
Make the home is as appealing as possible to entice all the available prospective tenants looking at that point. This will ensure you have a group of tenants to select from.

All tenants are looking for the best home, for the best price. The better your home presents, the more choices of tenants you will receive. The better the tenant you get.

A Quick Gauge

At a glance, I can tell if a property is asking too much or if I can make a profit. It is not a science – this is a quick / rough guess-timate that my mind immediately gauges before actually crunching numbers.

Example 1
Sales price $380,000   3brm

Average home in the area – similar but renovated-rent for $380-$400.

This roughly is a 5% return. (0.1% of the sale price)

A mortgage will be roughly $500 per $100,000. I round the price to $400,000 – monthly repayments roughly $2,000 per month (totally depends on your interest rate)

At $400 per week, x 52
                = $20,800   rental income
$2,000 x 12   = $24,000   mortgage due

This property is negatively geared, as you will need to put funds in to top up your mortgage.

** There is no freedom in the loan- you will have to continue to work to top up the balance after the tenant has paid.

Example 2
Sales price $320,000   3brm

Average rental for the 3brm - $420 per week

You can see straight away that the return is well over the 0.1% of the asking price – that's a good sign for positively gearing and receiving an income.

Mortgage is roughly $1500 pm.

At $400 per week   x 52 = $20,800
At $1500 per month x 12= $18,000

As you can see the tenant's payments cover the mortgage and you have a small residual left. This is still not positively geared.. though close to covering all the costs, the council and water rates – service to the land will be approximately $2,000-$4,000 depending on your local council's fee's. So, this would be neutrally geared.
It doesn't cost you anything to keep the property, which basically pays for itself.

You still receive no income and cannot quit work just yet!

Ok Example 2 – is the home we are looking for, but we need to ensure an income. It is neutrally leveraged at this point, how can we maximise the return?

Dual Income

This is the pivotal part of positively gearing a home… if you have a second income, you are then outlaying the cost of work, the return on the outlay is far superior to the existing loan.

For example, 3.

Sales price	$320,000
Rent	$420pw 2nd dwelling (13)
Granny flat build	$130,000 (appx)
Loan now **	$450,000 / flat rent $350 pw
Mortgage	$2500 pm (appx)
Income;	$3,336 pm

Now we are in the business of receiving an income from the rental. It may only be $200 per week, but if you have 6 properties @ $200 p.w = $1200 per week residual income.

(Learn the techniques and strategies to get the 6 properties – by reading part 2 in this series; "How to Build a Property Portfolio ~ The SMART Way")

Equity potential

Know how to calculate whether a property has potential to improve its equity[14] by doing home improvements or renovations.

This is also not an exact science – mod cons increase the home's value and therefore the equity you now own.

For example, 4;

Purchase home at	$320,000
Improvements -	New kitchen
	New Bathroom
	New flooring
	New blinds
	New Paint
	Air conditioning
	Heated flooring
	Any extension

The above improvements could set you back anywhere between $20k - $50k+

The average kitchen is valued at approximately $15k- $20k. The average bathroom is valued at $12-15k approximately. All the work pricing is dependent on quality & size, obviously. But did you know that the average sales price will diminish the poorer the home looks visually and the more repair work a home is seen to need. Do the work yourself and increase the sale price by $100k or more!

We live in a new age of modern homes and an easy life style. If a home is presented in a way that looks to be "move-in ready" the sale price will increase sometimes dramatically with buyers fighting over the property to secure it.

Homes that need a lot of work, regardless of the listed price being considerably less to compensate for the work needed, will usually be priced down enough for there to be a profit, hence why "flipping" a home is so popular today.

The average home needing a complete renovation should be about $100k-$150k under the market sale price for its finished equivalent. The work should be able to be done by roughly spending half of that amount, sometimes less if you do the work yourself, then when you flip the average profit is $40k- $80k+ after the work is done. (depending on costs)
Then if you are looking at home to purchase, look for the one that needs all the work, and it's finished equivalent to see what the buffer is.

For example, 5;

Sale price of	$320,000	3brm
	need full make over	
Comparable sale(15)	$450,000	3brm
	fully renovated	

Research what your investment would get if you were to sell it when you have completed the renovation work. Find out sale prices on similar fully renovated homes. Ideally on that example, the home cost you $320,000, the renovation cost $60k (appx) bringing your total spend to $380k the home is now sellable at the comparable properties price= $450k. In this example, you have just improved your equity by $70k!

This would mean, if the original bank lent you the $320k, reinspected the home with all the work complete, the value on record would increase to a fully renovated home's value. You still only owe the $320k (if you borrowed the whole amount & had renovation funds avail.)

So now with the bank, your loan is $320k, the value of your property is now $450k you have invested a further $60k(?) to renovate, and the bank now has an adjusted total for the value of the property. If you didn't borrow the $60k to renovate, that is also included as your equity in the value of the home. Then you owe $320k, but its valued at $450k, you now have $130k of equity in your investment. To learn how to use this equity to position you to become a multiple landlord with a property portfolio, you will need to get book 2 in this series. (If you borrowed the renovations funds, deduct also)

Another example of your equity for a dual dwelling property;

Example 6
Purchase ppty $320k   Loan $320k
Renovate $60k   Max rent $ 400 pw
New ppty price $450k Granny flat $130k

New loan amount $450k New rent $750 pw
New sale price $650,000-$700,000

Roughly spent $130k to put the 2nd dwelling (granny flat), the flat's value to build is averagely $150-$200k
Because of the work involved, the timeframe to complete & the hassle taken out of the build for the next buyer, your investment of $130k putting the granny-flat up will usually yield you an extra $50-$100k on top of the invested $130k.

Renovated sale price was $450k, add the G. Flat, brand new to the block, the value will be around $650k-$680k, then the equity for this home will now be around $200k+.

Also, a good note to mention is that if you were to sell the property with a dual rental return of $700-$750pw any investor looking to purchase your property will see this as a great return!!! Most investors (and agents) gauge their sale price based on the return (the same as a commercial investment). If the rental price is 0.1% of the sale price (ie; $700 pw = $700,000 sale price) this roughly equates to a 5-6% return, which is average for a property investment, and the next investor will set it up as a negative geared investment. You could see this property sell as much as $750,000 in the right market with that return.

**If you find yourself in this position – What do you do? Upon finishing your renovations and scope of building work, lease the properties and get a high return you can do 2 things: Stay or fold!
Stay & you can use the equity to buy the next property, or cash in, get the best sale price on offer, & cash.

If you have a loan for $320k, the renovation of $60k and the granny-flat build for $130k, your expenses totalled $510k. (Note this does not include mortgage repayments made, interest paid, stamp duty (taxes) paid, agents fee's etc. etc. that has also been spent-see exact expenses chapter)

 ** Note if you are going to decide to sell or keep -please see for financial professional to find out what taxes or losses you may have when selling an investment in your state.

Exact expenses

When gauging your estimates there are many shortfalls with the tallying of your profit. Such as

- Mortgage insurance
- Mortgage repayments
- Insurances
- Stamp duty (purchase tax)
- Agents fee's
- Inspection reports
- Legal representatives
- Rates due till next period (settlement)
- Rates during renovations
- Electricity – while renovations carried out
- Portable toilet (when bathroom out of order)

You need to be mindful of the mortgage repayments required while there are no tenants. The first month or two, the renovations will be carried out and therefore there is no income at this stage, you will need to include these payments into your expenses / outgoings to get a clearer and more precise idea of your real profit margin. If you have less than 20% deposit, in Australia, banks will charge mortgage insurance, not to cover you – but the bank! They will chase you for the balance owing should you foreclose, unless you declare bankruptcy! This can be a costly insurance and your broker should be able to give you an exact price depending on your deposit amount, remember to leave renovation funds available where needed.

NO FUNDS TO RENOVATE? Ok in the situation that you have no available funds after purchasing the home, you will need to make sure the home is liveable and rentable as is and most importantly, potential for dual occupancy. Prior to settlement, start advertising it to be leased. Get a good strong tenancy (term & amount) and after a few months with the property tenanted apply for a 2nd mortgage for the build of a granny flat or new dwelling. You will need to be able to service the new loan until it is completely built and leased, but most banks will make payments on your behalf to the builder proportionate to the work done, so the loan interest will not be charged in full until complete. Talk to you broker about loan options.

Oversight

When renovating there are also many small things that get missed that may cost initially with your first tenant
For example;

- Antenna – may need repair or replace
- Phone sockets – access points
- Keys maybe missing for existing locks
- A pest control

If you don't know the home and it was old & needing work, these above-mentioned things may also pop up as an expense at some point, or numerous other issues.

It is safer to add 10% contingency to any budget for these unexpected repairs that become shortfalls when you haven't set aside for "unforeseen" expenses.

Special notation;
**If you are purchasing a two-storey property, where it has been separated into two flats there are a few WARNINGS to look out for;
It may not be council approved, getting council approval may not be an option due to regulations (ask a builder)

Fire standards insist on each flat having two exits.

An upper flat with only one exit can be expensive to correct. The ceiling to ground and floor to upper may not be fire rated (also can be very expensive to do).

The flooring hasn't been prepared for multiple living- therefore is not sound proofed.

This will mean every time a tenant upstairs moves the tenant's downstairs will hear very clearly and can cause a lot of complaints.

Absolute worst-case scenario – The council can tell you to rip out kitchen & bathrooms, if no approval, or someone can get hurt in a fire or worse.

**Do extra homework in this case or walk away.

Chapter 4   Investment checklist

Renovation / Improvement chart:

RENOVATION / IMPROVEMENT CHART

Property Address: _____

Work required:	(circle appropriate)	*Est cost/quote*
Kitchen:	ALL	Cupboards Cooking appl Benchtops Doors	$_____
Bathroom;	ALL	Fixtures Tiling Bath toilet Shower / vanity	$_____
En-suite	ALL	Fixtures Tiling Bath toilet Shower / vanity	$_____
Flooring:	ALL	SQM: _____ Type: timb / carpet / Float/ Vinyl	$_____
Blinds/Shutters	ALL	Total no: _____	$_____
Painting	ALL	No Rooms; _____	$_____
Gyprocking / Plastering		No rooms: _____	$_____
Built in robes	ALL	Brm1 Brm2 Brm3 Brm4 Brm5	$_____
Electricals	ALL	Lights / Power points / Alarm / new wiring	$_____
Air conditioning		New install / Replace	$_____
Doors / Locks	ALL	Front Rear Glass sliding Brms/Int	$_____
Plumbing	ALL	Bathroom / Kitchen / Laundry /	$_____
Roof	ALL	Repair / Paint / Replace /	$_____
Tiling	ALL	Floor / Bathroom / Kitchen / Laundry /	$_____
Fence	ALL	Sq._____	$_____
Outside	ALL	Landscaping / General / Patio / Pergola /	$_____
Other		_____	$_____
Other		_____	$_____
Other		_____	$_____
Other		_____	$_____

================

Sub Total $_____

Add 10% for Contingency $_____

Total $_____

Filling out this chart will give you an ideal scope of work require for the purchase, and help you gauge what costs will be involved getting the property up to a good rental standard. (spare copies found in rear of book)

Add anything that has come up in the building report that may need attention in to the "other" section.

So now let's do a
Property Purchase checklist;

(tear out & workable charts at rear of book for your use)

Property Investment checklist:

Asking /
Sales price $_____   0.1% =$_____
        Avr. Rent $_____ Higher   Yes / No

Comparable sale price (fully renovated sales price) $_____
Improvement cost $_____ appx   Rent renovated $_____
Total Reno + buy $_____   Is the rent <more or > less   than 0.1%

Comparable sale price $_____ minus
Purchase price & renovation costs =$_____
                        ================
                        = $_____ Equity

Is there any equity to be made in this purchase when you have renovated?   Yes / No

======================= Able to positively gear? =======================

Can you build a 2nd dwelling / Get a 2nd income?   Yes / No
2nd dwelling potential   GF Cost $_____   Rent $_____ pw

Sales price for Similar home + G.flat $_____ (recent sale price)

Total GF Cost + Purchase + Reno $_____

                        ======================
                        $_____ is there Profit   Yes / No

Total rent house $_____ pw + flat $_____ pw = $_____ pw x 52 div 12 = $_____ -

Total mortgage with all expenses $_____   repayments pm; $_____

                        ===============
                        Is there a cash flow   Yes / No

                                    Amount $_____
$_____ cash flow pm, x 12 div 52 = $_____ Per week cash flow

                ** If you have answered NO to any of ^
                    Not a recommended purchase

The property investment checklist – is set for a positively geared property. This whole guide is based on purchasing a home with the aim to have a stream of weekly rental income after paying all expenses.

If you use the guide correctly, you should be able to gauge if the investment will suit your needs. (more copies available at the rear of this book, you can screenshot & print)

If you are looking to invest, and you don't need the dual income straight away, you can stop at the first section of the checklist.

If you neutrally gear your property and if don't have to pay much out of your pocket in expenses, it is also a great investment.

Best result would be, you buy a couple of properties and let the tenants pay them off, until you are ready to sell and keep the profits. If the market has moved there will be even more profit than what has been paid off the loan.

Negotiating / Securing a property

So, you've run some figures, made the decision to purchase this property, now you need to secure the deal and negotiate a price with the seller.

There are no hard & fast rules, every person is different and as I have been negotiating on behalf of many people, main rule is not to offend anyone! I have had sellers who refuse to sell to a buyer who had offended them with their original offer, which by law I have to submit!

I have had purchasers pull out as they didn't like the sellers negotiating tactics or refusal to budge of a price and walk away.

Different nationalities tend to have different customs when it comes to negotiating. Some are ruthless and offer ridiculously low, some laugh it off and pretend they were joking, just to see where it lands.

The selling agent has told the vendors (seller) what amount they should expect in the current market. Some agents may be wrong with their appraisal, but generally they work the area and know what similar homes are selling for. They then can't really advise an owner to take a much lower offer when its contradicts the advised achievable sale price originally given.

Always get your professional legal representative to look over the contract before signing, email it to them when you think this is the potential purchase.

The Buyers' Market

The Buyers' Market is usually caused when interest rates have increased causing buyers to hold off, or house prices have bubbled (seen excessive price increases) and the market has halted and prices recede. In a down turning market, as more homes come on to the market, and interest rates rise, buyers stop looking... available homes on the market become plentiful and the offers start coming in under the desired selling price. In this market, you can often go backwards & forwards for quite some time before agreeing on a price. The buyers' market is the best time to buy as you can get some really good deals as sellers become quite desperate.

The Sellers' market

In a Sellers' market – it is the complete opposite. You need to make good strong offers early & try to lock the vendor in to an agreed price before someone else comes along and offers more! When there aren't many properties available to buy and competition is getting strong you need to be in a position to crunch your numbers fast and sign the contract upon viewing the home.

Many times, I have seen people lose homes, trying to negotiate at the last stage, wanting to get a bargain and losing the whole deal to another buyer. If you would be happy to pay the price they are asking: pay it! The amount of buyers who come back a week later and say "I should have paid that... now I would pay $10,000k+ more", but it's too late. Don't kick yourself trying to save a few thousand dollars. Secure the home, make a good strong offer that you would be happy with, as close to the asking price as you can or you will have to keep looking!

Alleviate hard sales tactics

Real Estate Agents are renown for "stretching the truth" or not showing their whole hand, when it comes to negotiating.

I always make an offer on the home to the agent when inspecting a property to see how it lands. You will immediately be able to gauge if you are close or in the same ball park or possibly the owner is unrealistic.

This will also help condition the owner, if they receive the buyers' opinions on every inspection carried out, they can get a better idea of what the current market is roughly expecting to buy their home for.

All owners would like that little bit more, and in a sellers' market you need to offer it. If you need to lock in a property and you can see there are a lot of interested parties, offer full or above full price.

The agent has told their client a certain price to expect, and as they are professional, they will do their best to get their quoted price, more to satisfy the client and successfully make the sale with ease. If there are ample buyers the agent will hold firm to the price they are expecting, especially if that's what they have quoted the vendor.

You will generally be told the offer needs to be over $xyz, or they may tell you the figure of an offer that has been rejected. Some will tell you a price range, so between ___ & ___ or a good agent will just tell you they have had a better offer and that's it's too low.

I say a good agent, because their job is to get the best price for their client. If they tell you a price, you can go a little bit over and expect to get it for that price. When they leave it open, you have to increase your offer to a figure you are comfortable with, and that is usually over what the owner wants and the agent has got a good sale price for their client. This is not a bad tactic, it's a good selling agents' tactic, and the buyer is also happy as they have offered a price they are happy with.

An agent who is a good strong negotiator and holds firm to getting a buyer to offer their best price, is the type of agent you want to sell with. They are interested in getting the best price for their client, not just making a sale.

As you purchase or inspect prospective homes, keep an eye out for a good sales agent when you meet them. Although you may not buy off the best agent, you definitely want to sell with them. I have seen people get so much less than they should have, even up to $100,000 by using a poor agent and getting bad advice.

A good agent may be a higher sales commission, but think about this- at a higher commission it is in their interest to get more money for you, as their fee also increases. Stay away from flat fee agents. They are "flat fee" because they are a basic agent. There is no incentive for them to get you an extra $1,000 or $40,000. It may seem cheap when you are listing your home, but the difference between an average agent and a professional negotiator could see you achieve $50,000++ or more, for the extra $3,000-9,000 in commission they are definitely worth their fee and you will recoup it in the selling price.

Get your name listed with the agents in the area you are looking to purchase or appoint a buyers' agent (like me) for that area to help your search. You will be able to tell just from the properties marketing and meeting an agent and negotiating who is switched on.

Bad negotiators are great to buy off, so we like them too!

Special condition tip

One condition I request when making an offer that will secure the property, is access to the property pre-settlement. Many owners don't mind, especially if the home is vacant. Some solicitors advise their client against it, but if possible, access to start improving the home prior to the mortgage repayments starting is saving you money every day! If they don't allow you to start renovating and ripping things out, which, in fairness could devalue the home further, I ask to at least have access to start painting, and doing improvements only. That way the home is in better condition towards settlement.

They will ask you to take out insurance so they cannot be held responsible for any injuries or the like, and they also may ask for you to sign a disclosure that you take the home as is and agree to relinquish any issues with the condition of the home upon access.

Sometimes it may be wise to offer a small amount of rent for the access prior to settlement. Work out what the owner would be happy with, but the sooner you can access the property to start improving the quicker you will be able to lease the property once you own it.

Chapter 5

Project managing improvements

Now start the work, the renovation process

The Key is being organised and tradie ready! Estimates are done, you need to work out the order of trades people that need to work after or before one another to complete the job. Or you can appoint a project manager who handles renovations like myself, or a builder who will handle the whole renovation himself and get the trades he needs.

Make a list of the work required and try to put in priority order of work

For example;

> Demolish the old
> Strip the area: bathroom, kitchen etc.
> Electricals to be set
> Plumbing to be set, especially if moving
> Set blank canvas, re-sheet walls, paint
> Water proof wet areas
> Tile floors & walls
> Install cabinetry / vanity etc.
> Finalise plumbing
> Finalise electricals
> Install fittings; shower screens, benchtops etc.

Depending on what work you are doing, there will need to be an order to the list of work, so you can plan who comes first and which jobs need to be done before others can commence etc.

The TV shows that renovate a whole house in 1 week and have all trades in at the same time is crazy, somewhat unsafe and unrealistic.

Tradies need their work space and if possible some drinks & snacks! You will get happier tradesmen who appreciate your efforts and enjoy small appreciative gestures like the odd pizza, or a tea & coffee station!

Appointing trades

Once you figure out the order of the work required, you can appoint each trade. It is standard for them to ask for 30-40% cost upfront for materials, 30% half way and the balance upon completion or similar.

If you can try to appoint them all with a rough time frame they can "pencil" your job in. Some tradesmen, especially the good ones, are quite busy and managing the times that they are all available can be a huge headache later on, if they have taken on other jobs, you will be waiting for them to find time to fit you in which can be very frustrating and each delayed day costs you.

Timeframe Vs Costs

Trades people can sometimes delay work, and the costs can increase when you have no rental income yet.

Making sure all trades have your work required date, will ensure a smoother completion process, it doesn't always go to plan, but there have only been a few occasions a tradesman has had to delay or cancel a delay due to an emergency or one has not been able to come back and complete the shower screen for 2 weeks, other than that I run a tight ship with trades schedules and work dates. The more organised your plan is the better the process will evolve.

Chapter 6

Choosing a Property Manager

Who will look after your investment??
When looking for a property manager, or an
agency to look after your investment, you need
to be aware of a few things:

- Not all agents are invested in their job,
  PM's don't make large commission or
  get performance incentives, nor monthly
  quotas.

- Not all agents can negotiate with a tricky tenant or in difficult situations
- Not many agents will go above and beyond
- Not all agents will treat your home like their own
- Not all agents will care about relationships, or tenants!
- Not all agents have your best interest at heart

It is hard to find a good property manager. In my experience, the best are the go getters. The organised people who tackle issues head on and don't let problems fester and become major issues.

A good property manager has been in the job a few years, and has the experience to handle all situations.

Sometimes these property managers come across as "hard" or a little forceful. But they need to be, they have to ensure your rent will be paid regularly, and chase arrears to recover debt, if they don't care neither will your tenant.

I good way to gauge your local property managers is to get them to come and meet you at the property. Interview them as you would when getting a quote off a tradesperson.

Service expectation

Find out what you get for your management fee. Find out what arrears procedures they have in place, do they do 2-3 day arrears? You may think that is excessive but my team would do one day arrears, our aim was every tenant needed to be 7 days in advance at all times, if they have forgotten to pay, it is best you contact them straight away. That also lets the tenants know arrears are not tolerated and they will get into the habit of letting you know if there is any delay & that prevents them getting an arrears call!

How detailed are their tenant reference checks? Are references essential? Called?
Find out how systemised the office runs the rent roll. They need to be particular with their systems, organised, straight forward and have good switched on communication. You may not deal with only one staff member. Is there a high staff standard? Speak to a 2nd member of the team.

Call the office & check their response time. Pretend to be a tenant and make an enquiry on a property, ask if it is negotiable? Will they show you outside work hours? How responsive were they? Are they professional enough to handle your property, in all areas!

Ask them how often they do inspections and what their procedure is. They should at least inspect the property once within the first 2 months, then once 3 months after, so they have visited the tenant twice in the first 6 months, then once every 6 months for the first 2 years, then every 10 months, is acceptable, any less is not.

You should receive a detailed report and photos with today's technology.

Don't go with the cheapest agent- like sales agents if they are cheap they usually have a "care-free" system and cost you money. They will stick any tenant into your property.

A tenancy can cost you thousands with the wrong agent!

As they say; "pay peanuts & get monkeys !!"

Commissions / Fees

What's a fair price when paying an agent? You may be surprised to know that with the management fee there are also monthly & annual sundries to be paid! Such as bank fee's that are passed on, a statement fee for the monthly accounting and also the end of financial year statement fee, calculate & expect for it to total 10% approximately per annum.

Some agents here, especially in the outer regional areas or holiday lett areas charge 8% management fee + sundries + Tax. The average in a city suburb with a lot of competition is usually 5-6% + sundries, and the top agents at 7-10%! + Sundries!

If the tenant gets taken to a tribunal for a court order, or you change the tenant regularly, this fee could be as high as 15% of your total income. So, a cheaper agent will actually charge you more per annum to clean up the bad tenant that they put in!

Usually references weren't checked properly before entering into a lease, but they don't mind, it creates more work and income, that is also how they can charge a cheaper %, so shop around.

Don't forget you pay a week's rent every new tenant so it is in the agent's interest to change tenants often.

Ask for a 3-month trial agency agreement, or if you aren't happy with the agent, after entering into the agreement give notice and leave. The number of landlords that have had come to me saying they weren't happy and knew the agent was not doing their job properly and by the time the tenant moves out, they paid thousands in damages or loss of rent.

Getting a Grade-A tenant

80% of Tenants are every-day, people like ourselves who having a go at life, working, raising a family or trying to have a simple existence, happy to pay their rent and look after the home reasonably well.

10% Are habitual bad payers, don't look after where they live, sometimes drug addicts, party animals, disturb the neighbours, noisy cars, hoarders and the like. These are the worse-case scenarios, "avoid at all cost" tenants.

The last 10% of issues with tenancies arise from unforeseen circumstances. Like death in the family, loss of main income, sickness or family emergency. With the right agent, these are manageable issues that occur with some unsuspecting unfortunate people.

Reference checks are pivotal to ensuring a good tenancy. Previous rental history is essential for middle aged applicants who have never owned a home. Mortgage repayment bank account ledgers are sufficient for previous home owners. Parents can be on the lease guaranteeing the tenancy for first time renters.

Bad tenants sometimes declare their history is bad, usually they still owe money or they will try to hide the actual address and say they live with their parents or friend etc. Getting multiple bills & identification in the applicant's name will show any discrepancy with addresses.
I have caught out many applicants who are being terminated for severe arrears with another agent, they have put their friend as the "private" landlord. But us agents have access to listed sales & rentals records, and any good property manager will access these records to confirm ownership & agency details as standard

practise. If an agent manages the property they are usually listed as advertising the home at some point, and I call them.

Most tenants are your everyday citizens who would like to live in a decent place with some homely comforts and stress-free environment! Offering a home that has air conditioning or heating for colder climates today is essential. If the house gets too hot or too cold and there is no assistance they will shortly look for other accommodation so they don't have to endure another harsh season there. They can rarely afford their own system as cost of living is very high in western cultures (worse in others!), with no spare money or savings scarce, so they move.

Finding a long-term tenant who looks after the home is the ideal scenario, and though you can't guarantee life won't throw your tenant a curve ball, most hiccups in rental payments can be managed easily with a switched-on property management team.

Securing a good tenancy

Have a portion of control in your tenant selection. Request that the agent refers to you when they have an application, and find out about the history before agreeing on a tenancy, make sure thorough reference checks have been done.

If they have fair previous rental history, no damages claimed when they vacated the previous home, then there is no reason why you can't start the lease at 12 or 24 months. Many agents and landlords don't like to lock in for a long term as they can't increase the rent. Two years isn't such a long term that you would need to increase the rent. Securing a tenant for that period is a far smarter move and will guarantee there will be no period of vacancy for 24 months. That's securing your income!

Increase the rent

Unless interest rates have increased excessively, or you are financially struggling to secure the investment, I wouldn't recommend increasing the rent more than 5% every 2-3 years.

The average CPI(16) quarterly is 0.3-0.5%, annually hasn't been more than 2% for a very long time. Its hasn't been over 5% for a 5 years period since the 70's in Australia, which means although the rent needs to increase over a period of time, a tenant will feel more secure financially if there aren't too many increases and will stay longer.

Make sure when you do increase the rent, your property still remains cheaper than the competition available. Some Landlords keep increasing the rent and the market conditions have been stagnant for some time, a tenant will vacate for a cheaper property with similar amenities.

The last thing you want as an investor is to increase the rent $20 per week and risk having the home vacant & loosing 1 or 2 weeks rent.

If you look after a tenant, chances are they will be long term, and your investment will be hassle free.

Chapter 7

Financials & Paperwork

Every penny spent on your investment should be accounted for! All receipts, payments & outgoings including rates, insurances, service fee's & the like.

Also, you should keep a copy of the front page of the lease on hand and the agent will usually send you a copy and confirmation letter that the property has been leased, with the term and rental amount, ask for one if they don't.

One of the biggest "scams" I have seen with property managers, is to start the lease in the computer 2 weeks after the actual lease start date. This way they can pocket the 2 weeks cash in rent that has just been paid to them upon signing the lease and tell the owner it was vacant until the date that shows on the next statement. Getting a copy of the front page of the lease will ensure this doesn't happen. A tenant won't sign a lease and hand over two weeks rent with a lease that starts two weeks ahead, and you can be sure a tenant will always query when they see a copy of their ledger, where their first two weeks rent deposit is!

Each month you will receive a statement with the rent received & expenses paid on your behalf. Most agents can pay your rates for you at no extra charge, and forward water usage to the tenant for reimbursing.

It is definitely recommended to get landlord insurance, and shop around for the different policies available. I have dealt with many claims and unfortunately, that is when a landlord usually discovers they have a poor cover & the "terms" aren't exactly what were expected. One claim, the insurance was through the bank that had the mortgage, the condition was that all rent was covered above the bond. So, the bond was used for cleaning & damage's and the 3.5 weeks rent was the claim. They declined the claim, they didn't not cover for ANY cleaning nor damage. So, the 4 weeks bond covered the rent lost and there were no further monies to be claimed, be careful of fine print.

In Australia, my preferred Insurance is EBM, quite simply as they cover EVERYTHING and I have never had an issue with any claim, or fine terms clauses pulled out upon submitting a claim, and I have dealt with pretty much every insurance policy for Landlord cover that's exists (in Oz!).

Having your expenses itemised properly will ensure you are claiming correctly and assist your accountant working out the end of year financials.

There are many types of outgoings;
- Rates & levies
- Repairs & maintenance
- Refurbishments / improvements

This will help clarify what portion of the expenses can be claimed for the year, and possibly depreciation[17] your accountant can claim over the next 5- 8 years.

At the end of each financial year take all of your receipts, an itemised list of expenses and income to your financial accountant, Aka; Tax man.

Positively geared properties may mean you fall into a higher tax bracket. Most accountants advise to negatively gear your investment to take advantage of the tax breaks. Though this is surely a soft option, who cares if you pay more tax today when you are setting up your financial freedom by creating a residual income!

The following book in this series "How to Build a Property Portfolio~ The SMART Way" teaches you how to now build a Multi-million-dollar Property Portfolio, and retire on residual rental income!

Recap

So as a recap, here's the ideal points to take away from this book:

Educate yourself about your preferred area to buy in. Look for potential dual occupancy properties that have a second dwelling or have the ability to build a granny flat or second dwelling.

Refine a search on your real estate site, and on each word do a separate refined search: Dual income, Multiple income, Positively geared, Sleep out, granny flat, granny flat potential, self-contained, studio, in-law accommodation, positive rent return, high yield, flat potential, teenage retreat, pool house, 2nd dwelling, second dwelling,

The idea is for the rental return to cover the total outgoing costs and then give you a residual income.

Some properties will be cheaper as they are in need of TLC (tender love & care), or it may say renovators delight, these means your will need to do work, but you can create more equity improving the property.

If finances are lean, apply for the mortgage solely, renovate & lease out the original home, then secure a tenant THEN apply for a top up mortgage for the granny flat build.

Having the 1st tenant ensures the rent will service the original loan, applying later for the increase of your mortgage for the granny flat build will show surplus income from a 2nd rent once the flat is built and leased and the loan will be easier to secure.

This is assuming you have the renovation funds and granny flat build funds available!

But what if you don't...? This book has described how to improve the home to improve your equity, to do this you need to have funds available to proceed. When initially purchasing the property, you need to ensure the deposit you have will secure the loan and also some home improvements.

Be prepared to do the painting and handyman jobs, seek friends or family that may be able to help, if funds are scarce in order to save on costs. Get multiple quotes, barter or trade off your skills with your needed skill. (Do some work for a mate who can help your renovation)

Another option is that you could pay more for the initial purchase and buy a property not requiring renovation and get a better conditioned home and seek a loan for the flat build.

When looking at the purchase, and adding a granny flat build, you can approach your lending body to increase the mortgage to cover the build, as it will also achieve a rental yield. So, securing a tenant in the original property will make the 2nd loan application a lot easier.

Calculate your end costs against the rental yield after all expenses and only secure a "positively geared" property: that pays for itself as well as residual money each week as income to you.

Ensure you attract a good tenant and find a good reputable agent.

You can also find out more about managing a

property, in the book:
Self-Manage   The Smart Way
The Landlord guide to DIY Property Management

Property 💡 Smart

Appendix

(1) Positively geared – The rental income covers the whole expenses of the property
   a. You are in positive cash flow after all outgoings are paid

(2) Residual Income – Income after all expenses are paid, the balance paid to owner after the work is done (also see Passive income)

(3) Financial freedom – To be able to live comfortably without the need to go to work

(4) Buying Power – purchasing power, your equity and savings available to spend

(5) Positive cash flow – indicates liquid asset's, money available after expenses paid

(6) Capital Gains –profit from a sale of property

(7) Dual income- 2 incomes

(8) Negatively gearing- is financial leverage where a buyer's interest on the loan is more than the income

(9) Vacancy rates – The % an areas rental home are empty per annum /specified time

(10) Feasibility chart – degree of being easily done, achieved or reasonable

(11) Vendor – The owner of a property for sale

(12) Buyer's Market –a situation where supply exceeds demand

(13) 2nd Dwelling- second dwelling; flat, cabin, home, or other substantial structure

(14) Equity – value of worth in asset minus liabilities

(15) Comparable sale- a recent similar property sold in current market condition

(16) CPI- Consumer price index: the % of inflation on prices
(17) Depreciation: The accounting method calculating the cost of a tangible item over its deemed life span.

SARAHS
MANAGEMENT
AND
REAL ESTATE
TECHNIQUES

Property Smart

About the Author

Sarah Davis is a Licensed Real Estate Agent, Property Investment Guru, life coach, and Author who runs a boutique Buyers Agent & Property Management consultancy business on The Central Coast, NSW Australia, (1.5 hr nth of Sydney). She has been in the Real Estate game and an investor straight out of high school.

Sarah's business model is outlined in her book series "Property Smart". She advises clients on purchasing investments with the purpose of positively gearing the income, building the property equity and ensuring a residual income from the investment, for financial freedom!

As well as managing her residential rent roll, she re-develops properties, oversees new builds for multiple dwellings and secures dual occupancies both for her clients and herself.

Sarah gives down to earth advice to any property investor, so others can invest to retire simply by following her guidelines.
Look for the next "Property Smart" book in this series. These books aim to help people invest and set up financial security. The Property

Smart series shares great tips and inside information from an agent's perspective.

Or Follow Sarah on her Facebook page : Professional Buyers Agent & Property Management
https://www.facebook.com/buyersagentcc/
or her web page
www.buyersagentcc.com.au
Connect on fb
https://www.facebook.com/buyersagentcentralcoast
Sarah can also be contacted on
sarah@buyersagentcc.com.au

visit BOOK SERIES Page

at fb.me/PROPERTYSMARTBOOKS and

send messages to me

at m.me/PROPERTYSMARTBOOKS.

Please feel free to review the book,
Your feedback is always appreciated.

Look for more books in this "PROPERTY SMART series;

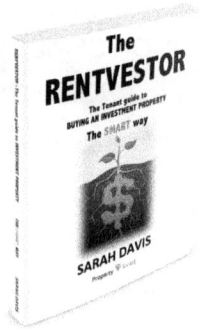

RENOVATION / IMPROVEMENT CHART

Property Address: _____

Work required:	(circle appropriate)	*Est cost/quote*

Kitchen: ALL   Cupboards   Cooking appl   Benchtops   Doors $_____

Bathroom;   ALL   Fixtures Tiling   Bath   toilet Shower / vanity $_____

En-suite   ALL   Fixtures Tiling   Bath toilet Shower / vanity $_____

Flooring: ALL   SQM: _____ Type: timb / carpet / Float/ Vinyl $_____

Blinds/Shutters   ALL   Total no: _____ $_____

Painting   ALL   No Rooms; _____ $_____

Gyprocking / Plastering   No rooms: _____ $_____

Built in robes   ALL   Brm1 Brm2 Brm3 Brm4 Brm5 $_____

Electricals   ALL   Lights / Power points / Alarm / new wiring $_____

Air conditioning   New install / Replace $_____

Doors / Locks   ALL   Front Rear Glass sliding Brms/Int $_____

Plumbing   ALL   Bathroom / Kitchen /   Laundry / $_____

Roof   ALL   Repair /   Paint /   Replace / $_____

Tiling   ALL   Floor /   Bathroom / Kitchen /   Laundry / $_____

Fence   ALL   Sq._____ $_____

Outside   ALL   Landscaping /   General /   Patio /   Pergola / $_____

Other   _____ _____ $_____

Other   _____ $_____

Other   _____ $_____

Other   _____ $_____

================

Sub Total $_____

Add 10% for Contingency $_____

Total $_____

Property Investment checklist:

Asking /
Sales price $_____   0.1% =$_____
         Avr. Rent $_____Higher Yes / No

Comparable sale price (fully renovated sales price) $_____
Improvement cost $_____appx   Rent renovated $_____
Total Reno + buy $_____   Is the rent <more or > less   than 0.1%

Comparable sale price $_____ minus
Purchase price & renovation costs =$_____
                          ==================
                          = $_____ Equity

Is there any equity to be made in this purchase when you have renovated? Yes / No

======================= Able to positively gear? =========================

Can you build a 2nd dwelling / Get a 2nd income?   Yes / No
2nd dwelling potential   GF Cost $_____   Rent $_____ pw

Sales price for Similar home + G.flat $_____ (recent sale price)

Total GF Cost + Purchase + Reno $_____ -

                          ======================
                          $_____ is there Profit   Yes / No

Total rent house $_____pw + flat $_____pw = $_____pw x 52 div 12 = $_____ -

Total mortgage with all expenses $ _____   repayments pm; $_____

                                        ===============
                                        Is there a cash flow   Yes / No

                                        Amount $_____
$_____ cash flow pm, x 12 div 52 = $ _____ Per week cash flow

**** If you have answered NO to any of ^
Not a recommended purchase**

RENOVATION / IMPROVEMENT CHART

Property Address: _____

Work required:	(circle appropriate)						*Est cost/quote*

Kitchen: ALL   Cupboards   Cooking appl   Benchtops   Doors $_____

Bathroom;   ALL   Fixtures Tiling   Bath   toilet Shower / vanity $_____

En-suite   ALL   Fixtures Tiling   Bath   toilet Shower / vanity $_____

Flooring: ALL   SQM: _____ Type: timb / carpet / Float/ Vinyl $_____

Blinds/Shutters   ALL   Total no: _____ $_____

Painting   ALL   No Rooms; _____ $_____

Gyprocking / Plastering   No rooms: _____ $_____

Built in robes   ALL   Brm1 Brm2 Brm3 Brm4 Brm5 $_____

Electricals   ALL   Lights / Power points / Alarm / new wiring $_____

Air conditioning   New install / Replace $_____

Doors / Locks   ALL   Front Rear Glass sliding Brms/Int $_____

Plumbing   ALL   Bathroom / Kitchen /   Laundry / $_____

Roof   ALL   Repair /   Paint /   Replace / $_____

Tiling   ALL   Floor /   Bathroom / Kitchen /   Laundry / $_____

Fence   ALL   Sq._____ $_____

Outside   ALL   Landscaping /   General /   Patio /   Pergola / $_____

Other   _____ _____ $_____

Other   _____ $_____

Other   _____ _____ $_____

Other   _____ $_____

================
Sub Total $_____

Add 10% for Contingency $_____

Total $_____

Property Investment checklist:

Asking /
Sales price $_____   0.1% =$_____
    Avr. Rent $_____Higher Yes / No

Comparable sale price (fully renovated sales price) $_____
Improvement cost $_____appx   Rent renovated $_____
Total Reno + buy $_____ Is the rent <more or > less than 0.1%

Comparable sale price $_____ minus
Purchase price & renovation costs =$_____
                   ================
                  = $_____ Equity

Is there any equity to be made in this purchase when you have renovated? Yes / No

======================= Able to positively gear? =======================

Can you build a 2nd dwelling / Get a 2nd income?   Yes / No
2nd dwelling potential   GF Cost $_____   Rent $_____ pw

Sales price for Similar home + G.flat $_____ (recent sale price)

Total GF Cost + Purchase + Reno $_____ -
                         ======================
                    $_____ is there Profit Yes / No

Total rent house $____pw + flat $____pw = $____pw x 52 div 12 = $_____ -

Total mortgage with all expenses $_____   repayments pm; $_____
                            ================
               Is there a cash flow   Yes / No

                         Amount $_____
$_____ cash flow pm, x 12 div 52 = $_____ Per week cash flow

                        ** If you have answered NO to any of ^
                        Not a recommended purchase

Property Address: _____

Work required:	(circle appropriate)	Est cost/quote

Work required: (circle appropriate)   *Est cost/quote*

Kitchen: ALL   Cupboards   Cooking appl   Benchtops   Doors $_____

Bathroom;   ALL   Fixtures Tiling   Bath   toilet Shower / vanity $_____

En-suite   ALL   Fixtures Tiling   Bath   toilet Shower / vanity $_____

Flooring: ALL   SQM: _____ Type: timb / carpet / Float/ Vinyl $_____

Blinds/Shutters   ALL   Total no: _____ $_____

Painting   ALL   No Rooms; _____ $_____

Gyprocking / Plastering   No rooms: _____ $_____

Built in robes   ALL   Brm1 Brm2 Brm3 Brm4 Brm5 $_____

Electricals   ALL   Lights / Power points / Alarm / new wiring $_____

Air conditioning   New install / Replace $_____

Doors / Locks   ALL   Front Rear Glass sliding Brms/Int $_____

Plumbing   ALL   Bathroom / Kitchen /   Laundry / $_____

Roof   ALL   Repair /   Paint /   Replace / $_____

Tiling   ALL   Floor /   Bathroom / Kitchen /   Laundry / $_____

Fence   ALL   Sq._____ $_____

Outside   ALL   Landscaping /   General /   Patio /   Pergola / $_____

Other   _____ _____ $_____

Other   _____ _____ $_____

Other   _____ _____ $_____

Other   _____ _____ $_____

================

Sub Total $_____

Add 10% for Contingency $_____

Total $_____

Property Investment checklist:

Asking /
Sales price $_____   0.1% =$_____
          Avr. Rent $_____Higher Yes / No

Comparable sale price (fully renovated sales price) $_____
Improvement cost $_____appx Rent renovated $_____
Total Reno + buy $_____   Is the rent <more or > less than 0.1%

Comparable sale price $_____ minus
Purchase price & renovation costs =$_____
                                 =================
                                 = $_____ Equity

Is there any equity to be made in this purchase when you have renovated?   Yes / No

======================= Able to positively gear? =========================

Can you build a 2nd dwelling / Get a 2nd income?   Yes / No
2nd dwelling potential   GF Cost $_____   Rent $_____ pw

Sales price for Similar home + G.flat $_____ (recent sale price)

Total GF Cost + Purchase + Reno $_____ -

                                 ======================
                                 $_____ is there Profit   Yes / N

Total rent house $_____pw + flat $_____pw = $_____pw x 52 div 12 = $_____ -

Total mortgage with all expenses $ _____   repayments pm; $_____

                                          ===============
                                          Is there a cash flow   Yes / No

                                          Amount $_____
$_____ cash flow pm, x 12 div 52 = $_____ Per week cash flow

                              ** If you have answered NO to any of ^
                                 Not a recommended purchase

Property Address: _____

Work required:	(circle appropriate)	Est cost/quote

Work required: (circle appropriate)   *Est cost/quote*

Kitchen: ALL   Cupboards   Cooking appl   Benchtops   Doors $_____

Bathroom;   ALL   Fixtures Tiling   Bath   toilet Shower / vanity $_____

En-suite   ALL   Fixtures Tiling   Bath   toilet Shower / vanity $_____

Flooring: ALL   SQM: _____ Type: timb / carpet / Float/ Vinyl $_____

Blinds/Shutters   ALL   Total no: _____ $_____

Painting   ALL   No Rooms; _____ $_____

Gyprocking / Plastering   No rooms: _____ $_____

Built in robes   ALL   Brm1 Brm2 Brm3 Brm4 Brm5 $_____

Electricals   ALL   Lights / Power points / Alarm / new wiring $_____

Air conditioning   New install / Replace $_____

Doors / Locks   ALL   Front Rear Glass sliding Brms/Int $_____

Plumbing   ALL   Bathroom / Kitchen /   Laundry / $_____

Roof   ALL   Repair /   Paint /   Replace / $_____

Tiling   ALL   Floor /   Bathroom / Kitchen /   Laundry / $_____

Fence   ALL   Sq._____ $_____

Outside   ALL   Landscaping /   General /   Patio /   Pergola / $_____

Other   _____ _____ $_____

Other   _____ $_____

Other   _____ $_____

Other   _____ $_____

================

Sub Total $_____

Add 10% for Contingency $_____

Total $_____

Property Investment checklist:

Asking /
Sales price $_____   0.1% =$_____
          Avr. Rent $_____Higher   Yes / No

Comparable sale price (fully renovated sales price) $_____
Improvement cost $_____appx   Rent renovated $_____
Total Reno + buy $_____   Is the rent   <more or > less   than 0.1%

Comparable sale price $_____ minus
Purchase price & renovation costs =$_____
                              ==================
                              = $_____ Equity

Is there any equity to be made in this purchase when you have renovated?   Yes / No

======================= Able to positively gear? =======================

Can you build a 2nd dwelling / Get a 2nd income?   Yes / No
2nd dwelling potential   GF Cost $_____   Rent $_____ pw

Sales price for Similar home + G.flat $_____ (recent sale price)

Total GF Cost + Purchase + Reno $_____ -

                              =====================
                              $_____ is there Profit   Yes / No

Total rent house $_____pw + flat $_____pw = $_____pw x 52 div 12 = $_____ -

Total mortgage with all expenses $_____   repayments pm; $_____

                              ===============
                              Is there a cash flow   Yes / No

                                   Amount $_____
$_____ cash flow pm, x 12 div 52 = $_____ Per week cash flow

                    ** If you have answered NO to any of ^
                          Not a recommended purchase

Thank you for reading this book
I hope you enjoyed it

SDavis

www.ingramcontent.com/pod-product-compliance
Lightning Source LLC
Chambersburg PA
CBHW060625210326
41520CB00010B/1481